Ukraine

Kaitlyn Duling

childsworld.com

Published by The Child's World®
800-599-READ • childsworld.com

Photography Credits
ID 124964658 © Scanrail/Dreamstime.com, cover, 1; ID 138150709 © Elina Litovkina/Dreamstime .com, cover, 1 (inset); Maximillian cabinet/ Shutterstock.com, 6; ZagAlex/Shutterstock.com, 7; AB Photographie/Shutterstock.com, 8 (gray wolf); David Havel/Shutterstock.com, 8 (red fox); volkova natalia/Shutterstock.com, 8 (dolphins); Hennadii Filchakov/Shutterstock.com, 8 (wild pig); Vladimir Konstantinov/Shutterstock.com, 9; fotoak/Shutterstock.com, 10; wedmoments.stock/ Shutterstock.com, 11; Galina Tiun/Shutterstock .com, 12; kibri_ho/Shutterstock.com, 13; Vitaliy Holovin/Shutterstock.com, 14; deniska_ua/ Shutterstock.com, 15; ioanna_alexa/Shutterstock .com, 16; Rybalka/Shutterstock.com, 17; Shchus/ Shutterstock.com, 18; Drop of Light/Shutterstock .com, 19; Romeo Rum/Shutterstock.com, 20; paparazzza/Shutterstock.com, 21; nesavinov/ Shutterstock.com, 22; Smile Studio/Shutterstock .com, 23; Andriy Blokhin/Shutterstock.com, 24; Serhii Shcherbyna/Shutterstock.com, 25; Stock Holm/Shutterstock.com, 26; home for heroes/ Shutterstock.com, 27; konstantinks/Shutterstock .com, 28; Gints Ivuskans/Shutterstock.com, 29; Volodymyr Nik/Shutterstock.com, 30

ISBN Information
9781503875937 (Reinforced Library Binding)
9781503876361 (Portable Document Format)
9781503876989 (Online Multi-user eBook)
9781503877481 (Electronic Publication)

LCCN
2025938593

Printed in the United States of America

About the Author

Kaitlyn Duling believes in the power of words to change hearts, minds, and actions. An avid reader and writer who grew up in Illinois, Kaitlyn loves to learn about countries around the world. She knows that knowledge is the key to a bright future, and wants to ensure that all children and families have access to high-quality information. Kaitlyn has written over one hundred books for kids and teens!

Cover: Lviv's Old Town is known for its history, rich culture, and beautiful scenery.

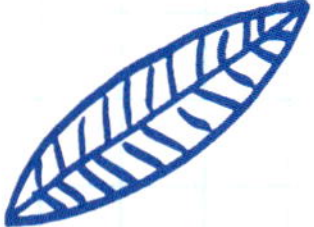

Table of Contents

Chapter One

Where Is Ukraine?

Imagine that you could float high up in the air. If you look down at the Earth, you would notice that the world has many land areas that are surrounded by water. These land areas are called **continents**. Many of these continents are made up of several different countries.

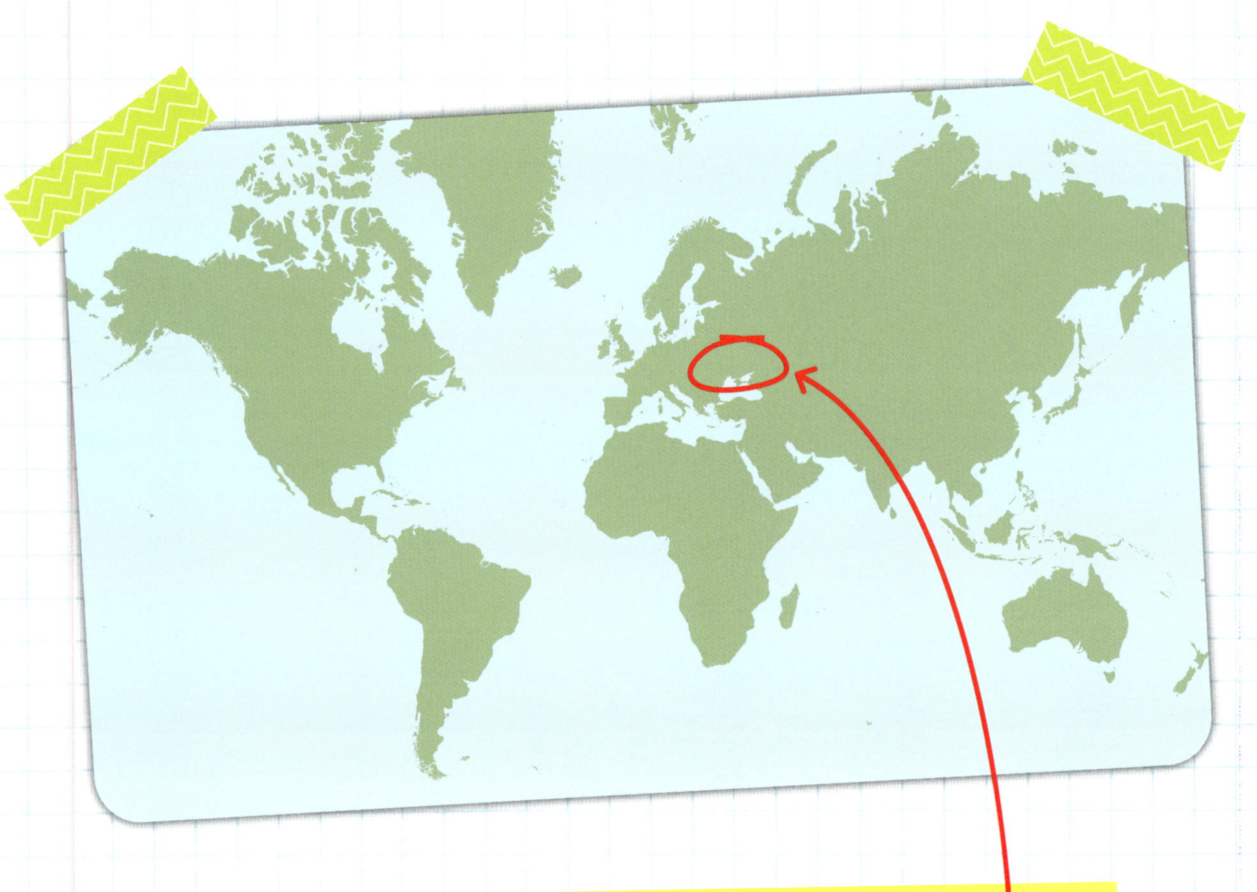

This is a flat map of the Earth. Ukraine is inside the red circle.

Ukraine is a beautiful country on the continent of Europe. It has flat **plains**, long rivers, and green forests.

Did You Know?
Crimea is on the Black Sea. It's claimed by both Ukraine and Russia. In 2014, Russian forces took over the area. The two countries continue to disagree over Crimea.

You will need to take an airplane to get to Ukraine.

Chapter Two

The Land

Much of Ukraine is made up of **steppes**. In the south, Ukraine has some mountains. They are part of the Crimean and Carpathian ranges. The highest mountain in Ukraine is called Hoverla (hoh-VER-lah).

The Crimean Mountains stretch along the coast of the Black Sea.

The flow of the Dnieper River is used for electric power.

Ukraine has several rivers. The Dnieper River is the longest in Ukraine. It is also one of the longest in Europe. It flows through Russia, Belarus, and Ukraine. Then it empties into the Black Sea. It stretches about 1,400 miles (2,250 kilometers)!

Did You Know?
Ukraine gets around 25 inches (63 cm) of rain each year.

Chapter Three

Plants and Animals

Many different kinds of animals live in Ukraine. Wolves, foxes, and wild pigs can be found there. Dolphins and porpoises live in the Black Sea. People can visit wild animals at Ukraine's many zoos. The Kyiv Zoo was founded in 1907. It is the largest zoo in Ukraine.

Gray wolf

Red fox

Wild pig

Bottlenose dolphins

The kalyna grows throughout Ukraine's forests. It's often featured in Ukrainian art and songs.

Ukraine is home to many flowering plants. For example, the kalyna (kah-LIH-nah) is a shrub with white flowers. It also has bright red berries. It is a popular **symbol** of Ukraine.

Chapter Four

Long Ago

The first people in Ukraine lived there thousands of years ago. Later, settlers arrived from ancient Iran, Greece, and Rome. Around 500 years ago, Polish invaders took control of the area. Later, Russia took control. Russian leaders banned the Ukrainian language.

A family picks vegetables from their garden in the 1950s. At that time, Russia had control of Ukraine.

Ukraine declared its independence in 1991, and the country elected its first president.

In the early 1900s, Ukraine became part of the Soviet Union. During World War II, the area was invaded by Germany. In 1991, the Soviet Union ended. Ukraine declared its independence! The country made its own laws, money, and official language.

Did You Know?
The Soviet Union was the world's largest country.

Chapter Five

Ukraine Today

In 2014, the Russo-Ukrainian War began. Russia and Ukraine were fighting over a piece of land called Crimea. Both countries wanted to control it. Later, more fighting broke out on the border between the two countries.

Mount Bolgatura is near the village of Gurzuf on the southern shore of Crimea.

Did You Know?
Since the Russo-Ukrainian War began, more than six million Ukrainians have left the country.

A destroyed Russian tank sits in the outskirts of Kyiv, the capital of Ukraine.

In 2022, Russia sent troops to fight in major Ukrainian cities. The war quickly spread beyond Crimea. Today, countries around the world are trying to end the war. They do not want it to spread into other parts of Europe. All around the globe, people want peace for Russia and Ukraine.

Chapter Six

The People

The years of war have been hard on people in Ukraine. Homes and schools have been destroyed. People have lost their loved ones. When there are attacks, people must go to a safe place. Some go in train tunnels. Others sit in basements. Some Ukrainians have chosen to leave.

Many roads and bridges have been badly damaged during the fighting in Ukraine.

Young people wearing traditional clothing celebrate their culture and history at a festival.

Ukraine has many different **ethnic** groups. More than three-quarters of people in Ukraine are Ukrainian. The second largest group is Russian. Most Russians live in northeast Ukraine.

Did You Know?
Ethnic groups in Ukraine include Belarusians, Moldovans, Crimean Tatars, Romanians, Roma, Poles, Bulgarians, and more.

Chapter Seven

City Life and Country Life

Ukraine has many large cities. The largest have tall buildings and streets filled with cars. Some have very old, beautiful buildings. Some are built on rivers or on the Black Sea. Most people in cities live in apartments. They ride buses and trains to get from place to place.

Kyiv is the largest city in Ukraine. It's located along the Dnieper River.

In central Ukraine, you can find traditional historic homes and villages.

Most Ukrainians live in cities. Some live in the country. In the steppe region, Ukrainians live in villages and on farms. They live in houses made of cement. Some live in **mazankas** made of wood, straw, and clay.

Did You Know?
Ukraine is the second-largest country in Europe, after Russia.

Chapter Eight

Schools and Language

In Ukraine, students go to school from ages six to fifteen. They learn things such as math, history, and art. In the upper grades, students study a special subject. They might choose languages, science, or something else. After they graduate, students in Ukraine can go to college. Students from all over the world move to Ukraine for college.

Children attend an event at their school in Dnipro.

Because of the ongoing war, many children attend school online or go to classes held in safe locations.

Most classes in Ukraine are taught in Ukrainian. Students in Ukraine sometimes learn English, German, or another language. Some schools used to teach in Russian. This has become less popular over time.

Did You Know?
Like in many countries, schools in Ukraine take a long break in the summer.

Chapter Nine

Work

Workers in Ukraine have many different types of jobs. In the country, farmers grow crops on large farms. There are also large **mines** in the country. Miners in Ukraine work with coal, nickel, and other minerals.

Ukraine has many valuable minerals. Mining is an important industry.

Workers assemble military equipment at a plant in Kyiv.

Cities in Ukraine have many factories. Factory workers build machines and goods. Some factories make chemicals. During the Russo-Ukrainian War, more workers became drivers and builders. Ukraine's military has around one million members. Soldiers fight in the war. Members of the military also work as doctors, lawyers, and more.

Chapter Ten

Food

Ukraine is famous for *borscht*. It is a soup made with beets. Beets and potatoes are both used in many Ukrainian dishes. They are grown in the country's rich, dark soil. Wheat and cabbage are often used in cooking, too.

Borscht is a traditional Ukrainian soup.

Varenyky is a staple of Ukrainian cuisine.

Another popular food in Ukraine is *varenyky* (vah-REH-nih-kih). This is a type of **dumpling**. They can be stuffed with potatoes or cabbage. And for dessert? Ukrainians love sweet cakes, like honey cake. Some people even make sweet varenyky. They are stuffed with berries or cheese.

Did You Know?
There are around 30 different kinds of borscht. Some are hot. Others are cold!

Chapter Eleven

Pastimes

Ukrainians love to have fun! Soccer is a huge sport in Ukraine. Wrestling and swimming are popular, too. In Ukraine, it is common to see people walking from place to place. City people walk along wide sidewalks when the weather is nice. They also have picnics in parks.

Young people in Kyiv enjoy the city's beautiful public parks.

You can see Ukrainian folk dancers as well as modern performers throughout the country.

Ukrainians like to celebrate their history. They enjoy **folk** dancing and folk music. There are several theaters and museums across the country. In the spring and summer, there are many festivals. It is easy to find things to do in Ukraine.

Chapter Twelve

Holidays

New Year's Day is a huge celebration in Ukraine. People throw parties and light fireworks. They also decorate trees. Easter is another popular holiday. On Easter, people decorate eggs with wax and bright colors. The eggs are called **pysanka** (pih-SAHN-kih).

Pysanka are beautifully decorated eggs. Some people believe that pysanka bring good luck, too.

People jump over flames during the Ivana Kupala holiday.

Ivana Kupala is a holiday that celebrates summer. On the night of June 23, people light fires. Then they jump over them! They also dance around trees and weave flowers into wreaths. Another summer holiday is Independence Day. On August 24, cities in Ukraine hold independence parades and parties.

Fast Facts About Ukraine

Area: 233,032 square miles (603,550 sq km); slightly smaller than Texas

Population: About 35,661,826 people

Capital City: Kyiv

Other Important Cities: Odesa, Kherson, Donetsk, Mariupol, Luhansk

Money: The hryvnia; one hryvnia is divided into 100 kopiykas

National Flag: Blue and yellow. The blue stripe represents the sky. The yellow stripe represents a wheat field.

National Holiday: Independence Day of Ukraine on August 24 (1991)

National Language: Ukrainian

Head of Government: The prime minister of Ukraine

Head of State: The president of Ukraine

National Song: Ukraine's national anthem, known as "Shche ne vmerla Ukraina," was adopted by Ukraine's government in 1991.

The glory and will of Ukraine has not yet perished,
And yet still upon us, Ukrainians, fate shall smile once more.
Our enemies shall melt away, like the dew in the sun.
And we too shall rule, O brethren, the homeland of our own.

Chorus:
Soul and body shall we lay down for our liberty,
And we'll show, O brethren, that we're a Cossack family!

Brethren, let's join in a bloody fight, from the Sian to the Don
Ne'er shall we allow others to rule in our native land.
The Black Sea will smile, and grandfather Dnipro will rejoice,
For in our own Ukraine fortune shall flourish once again.

Chorus

Our persistence and our sincere toils will be rewarded,
And freedom's song will resound throughout all of Ukraine.
Echoing off the Carpathians, and rumbling across the steppes,
Ukraine's fame and glory shall be known among all nations.

Chorus

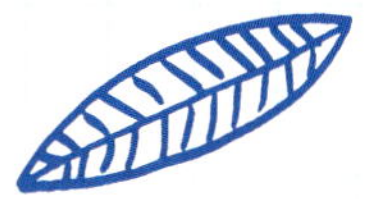

Famous People:

Oksana Baiul: figure skater

Milla Jovovich: actor, model

Volodymyr Khavkin: scientist who created an effective vaccine against cholera

Jan Koum: cocreator of WhatsApp

Maximilian Levchyn: entrepreneur, cocreator of PayPal

Golda Meir: fourth prime minister of Israel

Taras Shevchenko: poet, artist

Igor Sikorsky: inventor of the first helicopter

Elina Svitolina: tennis player

Lesya Ukrainka: poet, playwright

Svyatoslav Vakarchuk: musician, activist, soldier

Volodymyr Zelenskyy: president of Ukraine starting in 2019

Ukrainian Folklore:

The Bird's Gift
One day a little girl and her grandfather saw a bird freezing in an early winter snowstorm. The little girl gently wrapped the bird in her scarf and brought it home. All winter long, she and her grandfather took care of the bird. In the springtime, the bird was healed, and the girl set it free. Then one day the little girl and her grandfather found beautiful blue and gold eggs in the grass. They were a thank-you gift from the bird for their kindness. These were the first pysanka!

Volodymyr Zelenskyy

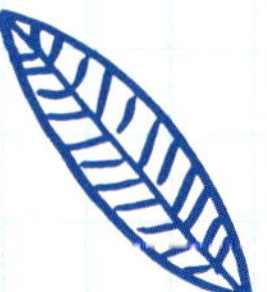

How Do You Say . . .

English	Ukrainian	How to Say It
hello	pryvit	pree-VIT
goodbye	do pobachennya	DO po-BAH-chen-ya
please	bud laska	BOOD LASS-kah
thank you	dyakuyu	DYA-kuh-yoo
one	odyn	oh-DIN
two	dva	DVAH
three	try	TREE
Ukraine	Ukraina	oo-kray-EEN-ya

Glossary

continents (KON-tih-nents) Earth is divided up into land areas called continents. Ukraine is a country on the continent of Europe.

dumpling (DUMP-ling) A dumpling is made of dough that has been boiled, fried, or steamed and has meat or vegetables wrapped inside. A varenyky is a type of dumpling.

ethnic (ETH-nik) Ethnic means having to do with a group of people sharing the same nationality, language, or culture. Ukraine has many different ethnic groups.

folk (FOHK) Folk means something that's traditional and belonging to the common people in a region. Ukrainians enjoy different types of folk dancing and folk music.

mazankas (mah-ZAHN-kahs) Mazankas are small houses found in the countryside. Some Ukrainians live in mazankas that are made of wood, straw, and clay.

mines (MYNZ) Mines are pits or tunnels where coal, gold, or other minerals are taken. Ukraine has a wide range of mineral resources.

plains (PLAYNZ) Plains are stretches of fairly flat land. Ukraine has plains, rivers, and forests.

pysanka (pih-SAHN-kih) Pysanka are decorated Easter eggs. It refers to a traditional method using wax where eggs are colored and decorated in intricate designs.

steppes (STEPS) Steppes are wide, treeless plains. Much of Ukraine is made up of steppes.

symbol (SIM-bull) A symbol is something that stands for an idea or value. The flowering plant called the kalyna is a popular symbol of Ukraine.

For More Information

READ IT

Davies, Monika. *Ukraine*. Bloomington, MN: Bellwether, 2024.

Doeden, Matt. *A Look at Ukraine*. Minneapolis, MN: Lerner, 2024.

Kesselring, Susan, and Elisa Chavarri (illustrator). *National Day Traditions Around the World*. Parker, CO: The Child's World, 2022.

Shaw, Mary. *Foods from Ukraine*. Parker, CO: The Child's World, 2024.

LOOK IT UP

Visit our website for lots of links about Ukraine:
childsworld.com/links

Note to Parents, Caregivers, Teachers, and Librarians: We routinely verify our web links to make sure they are safe, active sites—so encourage your readers to check them out!

Index